The Life of a
GRASSHOPPER

Clare Hibbert

Raintree

Chicago, Illinois

For more information address the publisher:
Raintree, 100 N. LaSalle, Suite 1200, Chicago IL 60602

Printed and bound in China by the South China Printing Company.

08 07 06 05 04
10 9 8 7 6 5 4 3 2 1

Library of Congress Cataloging-in-Publication Data:

Hibbert, Clare, 1970-
  Life of a grasshopper / Clare Hibbert.
      p. cm. -- (Life cycles)
Summary: A simple introduction to the life cycle of the grasshopper.
Includes bibliographical references (p.   ).
  ISBN 1-4109-0537-3 (hc)
 1. Grasshoppers--Life cycles--Juvenile literature.
 [1. Grasshoppers.]
I. Title. II. Series: Life cycles (Chicago, Ill.)
  QL508.A2H53 2003
  595.7'26--dc21

                    2003006586

Acknowledgments
The publishers would like to thank thefollowing for permission to reproduce photographs: p. 4 S. & D. & K. Maslowski/FLPA; pp. 5, 17 Robin Chittenden/FLPA; pp. 8, 10 Oxford Scientific Films; pp. 9, 26 Chris Hellier/Corbis; p. 11 A. R. Hamblin/FLPA; p. 12 Ken Preston-Mafham/Premapphotos; p. 13 Bob Gibbons/Ardea; p. 14 Borrell Casals/FLPA; p. 15 Simon Hoskin/FLPA; p. 16 Stephen Dalton/ NHPA; p. 18 Imagebank/Getty Images; p. 19 D. Malowski/FLPA; p. 20 Ecoscene; p. 21 A. Calegari/Panda/FLPA; p. 22 Eric Soder/NHPA; pp. 23, 24 Ron Austing/FLPA; pp. 25, 29 LarryWest/FLPA; p. 27 J. C. Allen/FLPA; p. 28 Mark Newman/FLPA

Cover photograph of a grasshopper, reproduced with permission of Premaphotos Wildlife.

The publishers would like to thank Janet Stott for her assistance in the preparation of this book.

Every effort has been made to contact copyright holders of any material reproduced in this book. Any omissions will be rectified in subsequent printings if notice is given to the publishers.

Contents

Any words appearing in the text in bold, **like this,** are explained in the Glossary.

The Grasshopper

Grasshoppers belong to a family of animals called **insects.** Other insects include bees and ladybugs. Like all insects a grasshopper has three parts to its body and three pairs of legs. The back legs are strong and powerful. The grasshopper uses them for jumping. Adult grasshoppers also have two pairs of wings for flying.

feeler

head

The three main parts of an insect's body are its head, thorax, and abdomen.

thorax

wing

leg

abdomen

Growing up

Just as you grow bigger year after year, grasshoppers grow and change, too. Different types of grasshoppers grow at different speeds, but they all go through the same changes. The different stages of the grasshopper's life make up its **life cycle.**

This adult grasshopper is resting on a stick.

Where grasshoppers live

Grasshoppers are found in almost every part of the world, especially in warm places. The place where an animal lives is called its **habitat.** Fields and grasslands are good habitats for grasshoppers. There is plenty of food to eat and plenty of places to hide.

A Grasshopper's Life

The grasshopper's **life cycle** begins in late summer when a female grasshopper lays her eggs. Inside each egg, a baby grasshopper develops. While it is inside the egg, the grasshopper is called an **embryo.** When spring comes, the egg **hatches.** A young grasshopper, called a **nymph,** comes out of it. It looks a little like an adult, but it is smaller and does not have wings.

From nymph to adult

Over the next month or so, the grasshopper nymph sheds its skin, or **molts,** about five times. Each time, the nymph's body looks more like an adult's. Once the **insect** becomes an adult, it can fly and it can **reproduce**—that is, make its own baby grasshoppers. A grasshopper's life as an adult lasts only a month or two.

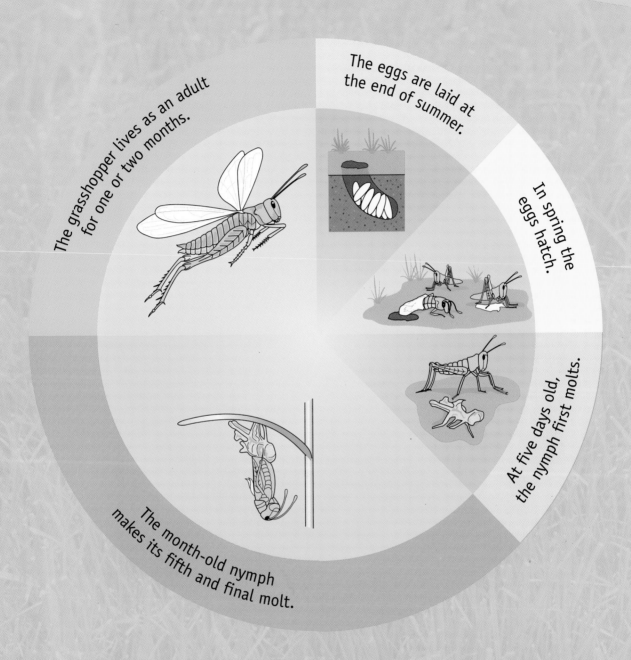

The eggs are laid at the end of summer.

In spring the eggs hatch.

At five days old, the nymph first molts.

The month-old nymph makes its fifth and final molt.

The grasshopper lives as an adult for one or two months.

This diagram shows the life cycle of a grasshopper, from egg to adult.

Hidden Eggs

Grasshopper eggs are laid at the end of summer. The female grasshopper pushes the end of her body into the soil and lays some eggs. She might lay as few as 6 eggs or as many as 150. They are stuck together in a kind of foam. The foam hardens into a sausage shape called a **pod.**

Once the egg pod has hardened, it is waterproof. The pod acts as a raincoat for the eggs inside.

Egg action

Each egg is about a quarter of an inch long—smaller than a pea. The inside is mostly **yolk.** This is food for the growing **embryo.** The embryo grows until it fills almost the whole egg. Then, winter comes and the soil around the pod gets very cold. The embryos stop growing. They are dormant—in a sort of sleep—until the spring.

A grasshopper could not live through the cold winter. The eggs hatch in spring, when all the snow has melted.

Pod snack

Not all the eggs make it through winter. Some pods are eaten away from the inside by tiny wasps and flies, whose parents burrowed into the soil and laid their eggs inside the grasshopper's eggs. Others are munched by beetle **grubs** in the soil, or dug up by hungry field mice and frogs.

Hatching

In spring, the snow melts and the soil warms up. The warmth wakes up the **embryo.** It finishes growing. Now it has been inside the egg for ten months. It fills the whole egg and is ready to **hatch.** All the eggs in the **pod** hatch in the same few minutes.

These nymphs are hatching out of their eggs.

On the move

The grasshopper youngsters are called **nymphs.** Each one is wrapped in a kind of skin. It wriggles up through the soil, then rolls around on the ground to shake off the skin. The nymph's body is soft, but it soon becomes hard in the sun. Now the nymph jumps away quickly, before ants and other hunters find it.

These wood ants are dragging a dead grasshopper back to their nest.

Ant attack

Ants are **insects** that live together in groups. They are **predators,** which means that they hunt and eat other animals for food. Working together, the ants attack and eat grasshopper nymphs. They have very sharp jaws for biting.

Mini Hopper

By the time the **nymph** is about five days old, its skin is too tight, just like clothes that you have grown out of. This is no problem for the nymph. The tight skin simply splits and peels off. It looks like a papery grasshopper ghost.

Underneath, the nymph has a brand new skin. This one has more room in it for the growing nymph.

This grasshopper nymph is between molts.

Molting

On its journey from nymph to adult, the grasshopper will shed its outer skin about five times. This is called **molting.** Molting happens every five days or so.

Changing insects

Young grasshoppers look a lot like their parents. To turn into adult grasshoppers, they only have to change a little. It's not the same for all **insect** young. Caterpillars look nothing like their adult form, butterflies. Their bodies change completely.

The nymphs look like their parents, but they are smaller and they do not have wings.

Growing Up

Like you, the **nymph** needs food to grow up big and strong. It starts eating right after it is born and keeps eating more and more as it grows. Most grasshoppers eat only plants, but some snack on crunchy **insects,** too.

Can you guess from its name what a grasshopper likes eating best of all? Its favorite foods are grasses. They include farmers' crops, such as wheat, barley, corn, rye, and oats.

The nymph has powerful jaws for biting through grasses and leaves.

Top teeth

The leaves of grass plants are tough and stringy. It is amazing that a grasshopper can munch through them, but it has the right jaws for the job.

Grasshoppers have strong mouthparts that can bite down hard enough to chew the leaves.

Sweet corn

Grasshoppers love corn. They eat the stems, leaves, and corn kernels. Corn is a living thing with its own **life cycle.** This sweet corn ripens in the summer sun.

Hop to Eat

For the first four weeks of life, the grasshopper **nymph** cannot fly, but it can move quickly. It jumps from plant to plant in search of food. With its long, strong back legs, the grasshopper can leap 20 times its own body length. If you could jump as well as a grasshopper, you would be able to leap over seven cars parked end to end!

Blast off! The nymph's powerful legs launch it into the air.

Long legs

Most of the time, the grasshopper's back legs are folded. To jump it straightens them out and pushes down at the same time. This action makes it spring through the air. When they are straightened out, the legs measure about as long as your little toe—twice as long as the grasshopper's other legs.

Muscle power

Muscles are stretchy tissues attached to the bones inside every animal's body, including yours. They pull on bones so that we can move. Grasshoppers have very strong muscles in their thighs that make their legs work. The muscles work best when they are warm. That is why grasshoppers like to bask in the sun.

This grasshopper nymph is sunbathing to warm up its muscles.

Danger All Around

By the time it is one month old, the **nymph** is nearly an adult. Of course, the bigger it grows, the more of a juicy meal it makes. Snakes, toads, and birds are all **predators** that like to eat young grasshoppers. There are **insect** predators, too, such as the praying mantis.

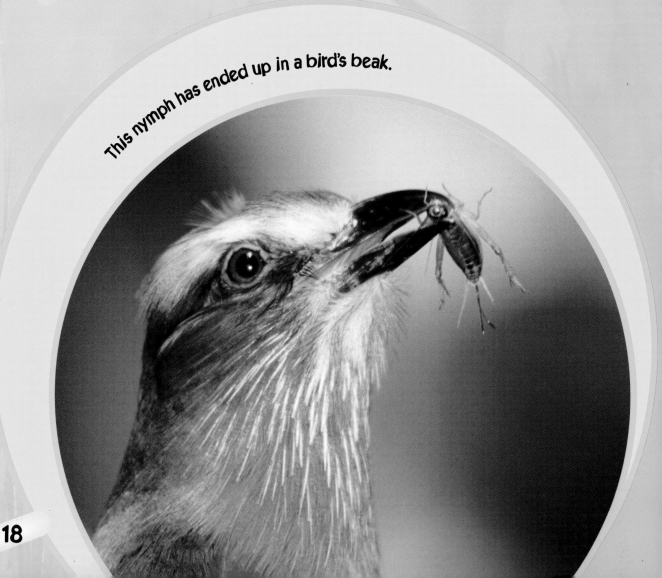

This nymph has ended up in a bird's beak.

Spitting mad

The nymph usually jumps to escape. Sometimes, though, it stays put and spits! No one really knows why it does this. Perhaps it is trying to confuse the predator.

A praying mantis prepares to attack this grasshopper.

Blending in

The nymph is hard to spot because it is green, like the grass. This is called **camouflage.** Some of the predators that eat grasshoppers use the same trick. The grass snake and the praying mantis are both green, too.

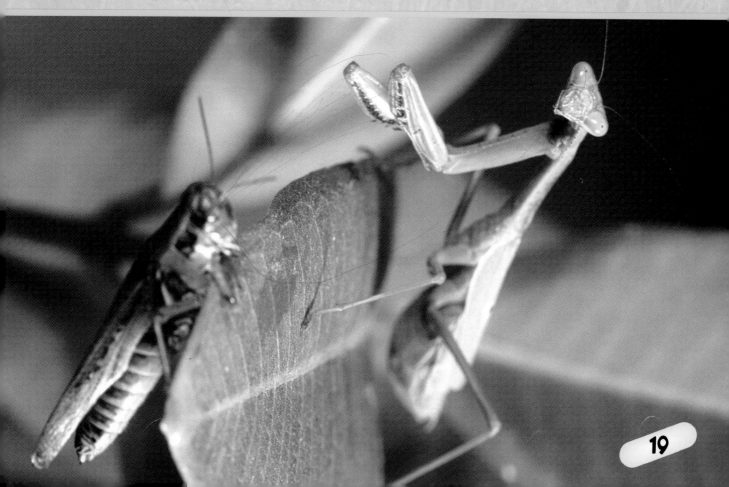

Up, Up, and Away

When the **nymph** is about 30 days old, it wriggles out of an old, tight skin for the last time. Underneath is its adult body, with wings that allow it to fly. The adult grasshopper has two sets of wings. The outer pair are tough, like leather. They protect the delicate flight wings underneath.

This grasshopper is just finishing its final molt. It is now an adult with wings.

First flight

The new adult grasshopper launches itself with a jump. As it zooms through the air, its wings start to beat very fast. Soon, it is flying for the first time.

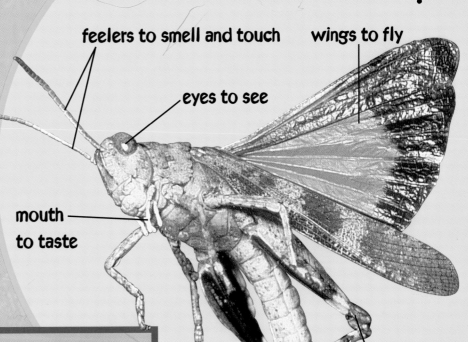

This grasshopper has ...

feelers to smell and touch

wings to fly

eyes to see

mouth to taste

ears on its knees

Senses

You know about the world by seeing, hearing, touching, smelling, and tasting. These are your senses. The grasshopper has senses, too. It has **feelers** for smell and touch. Its mouth tastes. It sees with its eyes but, unlike you, it has five of them. Finally, the grasshopper has ears, but not where you'd expect—many types have ears on their knees!

Finding a Mate

Now it is summer. For the first few days of being an adult, a female grasshopper is not ready to **mate.** The **egg placer** at the end of her body is still growing. Once it has finished developing, she is ready to mate.

This male grasshopper is singing to attract a mate.

Sweet sounds

Finding a male is not hard, because males make a chirping noise. You may have heard one when you were out walking in a park or a field. All the female grasshopper needs to do is follow her ears.

Some male grasshoppers rub their front wings together to produce their song. Others scrape their back leg against one wing, like a violinist uses a bow.

Grasshoppers are not the only insects that sing. The loudest is a type of bug called the cicada.

All kinds of songs

A male grasshopper can sing three different songs. The first is to attract females. When a female is interested, he chirps another song, to encourage her to mate with him. He also has a song for other males, telling them to stay away.

Future Nymphs

When they have found each other, the male and female grasshoppers **mate.** The male **fertilizes** the female's eggs. Now the eggs will be able to develop into **embryos** and, eventually, **hatch** into **nymphs.**

The female pushes her egg placer down into the ground and lays her eggs.

Laying eggs

The female only needs to mate once in her life. After this, all the hundreds of eggs in her body are ready to be laid. She spends the rest of her life—a month or two—finding good places to lay the eggs. She lays groups of eggs in different places and then leaves them. As well as hiding the **pods** in the ground, she lays some in the stems of grasses. Many of the egg pods will be eaten by **predators,** but some will survive the winter.

Grasshoppers can lay their eggs in sand as well as in soil.

Hard Times

Most grasshopper adults spend their short lives alone, apart from the time they **mate.** That can all change, however, when there is not much food around. Then, grasshoppers may band together in enormous groups called swarms.

This is a swarm of locusts. Locusts are a type of grasshopper.

Plague of locusts

The type of grasshopper that is best known for swarming is the locust. One of the largest swarms was in the United States in 1988. About 150 billion locusts came together and ate everything in sight. The area they covered was as big as 250,000 football fields. Many farmers' crops were ruined.

Killer sprays

Farmers do not like grasshoppers because they eat their crops. Some farmers spray their crops with special **insect**-killing chemicals. The sprays are called insecticides. Some farmers try to get rid of the grasshoppers another way, by putting animals that eat grasshoppers, such as chickens or ducks, in their fields.

Summer's End

Usually a grasshopper's adult life lasts only through a summer, a couple of months. Many grasshoppers are caught and eaten by **predators.** Those that last the summer start to die off when the fall arrives. The grasshopper's **muscles** won't work in the cold weather and there are not enough green shoots to eat.

In the fall, the grass starts to die off. There is not a lot of food for grasshoppers to eat.

Final feast

When the grasshopper dies, other **insects,** such as flies and beetles, move in to eat its body. All the food and energy that went into building the grasshopper's body does not go to waste.

Already, under the soil, **embryo** grasshoppers are starting to grow, ready to begin the **life cycle** all over again.

A robber fly's favorite foods are small wasps and bees, but it will also gobble up the body of a dead grasshopper.

Find Out for Yourself

The best way to find out more about grasshoppers is to watch them in the wild—look and listen for them in fields. Or you might also see grasshoppers in the zoo, in the insect house.

Books to read

Greenaway, Theresa. *Minipets: Grasshoppers and Crickets*. Chicago: Raintree, 1999.

Theodorou, Rod. *Animal Young: Insects*. Chicago: Heinemann Library, 1999.

Using the Internet

Explore the Internet to find out more about grasshoppers. Websites can change, and if some of the links below no longer work, don't worry. Use a search engine, such as www.yahooligans.com, and type in keywords such as "grasshopper," "locust," and "life cycle."

Websites

http://www.kidcyber.com.au/topics/grasshops.htm
Find facts about grasshoppers and some great photos, too.
http://www.enchantedlearning.com/subjects/insects/orthoptera/grasshopperprintout.shtml
More facts about grasshoppers, plus a picture to print out, label, and color in.

Disclaimer
All the Internet addresses (URLs) given in this book were valid at the time of going to press. However, due to the dynamic nature of the Internet, some addresses may have changed, or sites may have ceased to exist since publication. While the author and publishers regret any inconvenience this may cause readers, no responsibility for any such changes can be accepted by either the author or the publishers.

Glossary

camouflage coloring or marks on an animal that allow it to hide from predators

egg placer pointy end of a female insect's body that is used to lay eggs

embryo baby animal before it has hatched from an egg or been born

grub young insect that looks nothing like its parent. Adult insects have six legs, whereas grubs usually have none.

feelers also called antenna. Long horns that stick out from an insect's head that are used to sense the world around it.

fertilize to join together male and female parts to create the beginnings of a new living thing

habitat place where an animal lives

hatch when a young animal comes out of its egg

insect animal that, as an adult, has three parts to its body, three pairs of legs and, usually, two pairs of wings. Grasshoppers, beetles, and butterflies are all insects.

life cycle all the different stages in the life of a living thing, such as an animal or plant

mate when a male and female animal come together to make eggs or babies

molt to shed a whole layer of skin at a certain time in the life cycle

muscle stretchy tissue inside the body that allows an animal to move

nymph young insect that is similar to its parent, but will change to reach its adult form

pod casing that contains a grasshopper's eggs

predator animal that hunts other animals and eats them for food

reproduce to make babies, eggs, or seeds. Adult animals and plants are able to reproduce.

yolk part of an egg that contains food for the growing embryo

Index